William L Mactier

A Sketch of the Musical Fund Society of Philadelphia

Read Before the Society January 29, 1885

William L Mactier

A Sketch of the Musical Fund Society of Philadelphia
Read Before the Society January 29, 1885

ISBN/EAN: 9783337008710

Printed in Europe, USA, Canada, Australia, Japan

Cover: Foto ©ninafisch / pixelio.de

More available books at **www.hansebooks.com**

A SKETCH

OF THE

MUSICAL FUND SOCIETY

OF

PHILADELPHIA.

READ BEFORE THE SOCIETY JANUARY 29, 1885,

BY

WILLIAM L. MACTIER.

ORGANIZED FEBRUARY 29, 1820.
INCORPORATED FEBRUARY 22, 1823.

PHILADELPHIA:
PRESS OF HENRY B. ASHMEAD,
1102 AND 1104 SANSOM STREET.
1885.

MUSICAL FUND SOCIETY,

PHILADELPHIA.

PHILADELPHIA, Dec. 15, 1884.

WILLIAM L. MACTIER, ESQ.

DEAR SIR:

At the stated meeting of the Board of Managers of the Musical Fund Society, the President stated that you had prepared a short sketch of the musical history of the Hall. It was therefore resolved that you should be invited to read it before the Board, the members of the Society, the press, and a few other guests, at such time as you may select; and that, on the evening so chosen, the improvements in the Hall be open for public inspection. I would be glad to hear from you on the subject.

Yours truly,

JOSEPH G. ROSENGARTEN,
· *Chairman Committee of the Fund.*

PHILADELPHIA, Jan. 15, 1885.

JOSEPH G. ROSENGARTEN, ESQ.,
Chairman Committee of the Fund.

DEAR SIR:

I have your favor of 15th ultimo, enclosing a copy of the Resolution of the Board, at its last meeting, inviting me to read before the members of the Society, the press, and a few other guests, "A Sketch of the Musical Fund Society of Philadelphia."

It will give me great pleasure to do so, and, if agreeable to you, I would name Thursday evening, the 29th inst., for that purpose.

Yours very truly,

WILLIAM L. MACTIER,
132 Walnut Street.

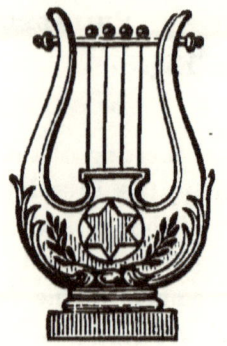

A SKETCH

OF THE

MUSICAL' FUND SOCIETY

OF PHILADELPHIA.

THE Musical Fund Society of Philadelphia was established February 29, 1820. It embraced professors of music and amateur members. The first meeting took place at Elliott's Hotel, Chestnut Street, January 7, 1820; Dr. Wm. P. Dewees in the chair and John K. Kane, Secretary. The officers were a President, Vice-President, Treasurer, Secretary, twelve Managers of the Fund, and twelve Directors of the Music. At the expiration of the year the Society, finding the room first selected for the accommodation of its members too small, took the Carpenters' Company Hall, on Chestnut Street, between Third and Fourth Streets. The practicings were held regularly on the first and third Thursdays of the month, and on the intervening Thursday evenings there were private vocal rehearsals, to which performing members only were admitted.

The objects of the Society were, first, to cultivate

and diffuse a musical taste; and secondly, to afford
relief to its necessitous professional members and
their families.

Its first concert was given on Tuesday, April 24,
1821, at Washington Hall, Third Street above Spruce
Street. The orchestra and chorus consisted of one
hundred performers.

The following is the programme:

MUSICAL FUND SOCIETY

OF PHILADELPHIA.

· FIRST CONCERT,

FOR THE BENEFIT OF THE FUND.

The public are respectfully informed that the First Concert
for the Benefit of the Fund will be given at the Grand Saloon,
Washington Hall, on Tuesday, 24th April, 1821.

Conductors—Messrs. B. Carr, B. Cross, P. Gilles, C. F. Hupfeld, T. Loud, G. Schetky.

PLAN OF THE CONCERT.

PART FIRST.

Overture—De l'Opéra Les Deux Aveugles de To-
    lède, full orchestra, ... *Mehul.*
Chorus—See, the Conquering Hero comes, . . . *Handel.*
Concerto Violoncello—Mr. Gilles, ... *Platel.*
Glee and Chorus—Awake, Eolian Lyre, with or-
    chestra accompaniments, by B. Carr, . . . *Danby.*
Grand Sinfonia in C, ... *Beethoven.*

PART SECOND.

Concerto, Violin—Mr. C. F. Hupfeld, . . . *Kreutzer*.

New Glee and Chorus—Sequel to the "Red Cross
    Knight," never performed in this country, with
    orchestra accompaniments, by B. Carr, . . *Dr. Clarke.*

Overture—De l'Opéra Tancredi, ... *Rossini.*

Chorus—Te Deum Laudamus, full orchestra ac-
    companiments, by B. Carr, ... *Graun.*

Grand Sinfonia in E, ... *Romberg.*

Leader—Mr. C. F. Hupfeld.

Principal Violins—Messrs. N. De Luce, Heinrich, Kalm, Getze, Grelaud, etc., etc.

Principal Violoncello—M. P. Gilles.

Violoncellos—Messrs. Lomman, Sr., etc., etc.

Tenors—Messrs. Cantor, C. Homman, etc., etc.

Principal Double Bass—Mr. Schetky.

Double Basses—Messrs. J. C. Homman and Klemm.

Principal Flute—Mr. Dannenberg.

The Conductors of the Vocal Music will alternately preside at the Organ.

The Orchestra will consist of one hundred Vocal and Instrumental performers.

To commence at 7 o'clock.

The members of the Society will please to apply at the Society's Hall, in Carpenters' Court, for their *two Ladies' Tickets*, on Saturday, Monday and Tuesday, from nine till one o'clock.

Tickets, one dollar each, for sale at the music stores of Messrs. G. E. Blake, G. Willig, Bacon & Hart, Klemm & Brother, and at the book stores of Messrs. M. Carey Son, M. Thomas, and at the Washington Hall on the evening of the performance.

April 20.

In order to secure the proper rendition of the concerts, the Society began the formation of a musical
library, and large sums of money were appropriated
to the purchase of sheet music, opera scores and musical instruments. The catalogue of printed music,
made up during the year 1879, numbered 304 pieces,
comprising overtures with full orchestral parts, opera
music, oratorios, sacred music, symphonies with orchestral parts, and miscellaneous pieces.

The most distinguished and estimable of our citi-
zens rapidly joined the Society and became interested
in its advancement. Its first President was Dr.
William P. Dewees, and its first Vice-President Dr.
Robert M. Patterson. Judge John K. Kane, Benjamin Say, Francis Gurney Smith, Franklin Peale,
Dr. R. La Roche, Francis M. Drexel, Dr. George
McClellan, Thomas Sully, John Keating, Jr., William
Meredith, James Nevins, William Kneass, John F.
Grelaud, Dr. Isaac Hays, Abraham Ritter, and Francis Hopkinson, became members in 1820. A peculiar
feature of the Society was the admission of a large
number of lady members, both amateur and professional. At the meeting, April 4, 1820, at 154 Chestnut Street, Dr. Wm. P. Dewees, President, in the
chair, there were elected four gentlemen, three lady
amateurs and two lady professors.

June 10, 1822, the Society gave Haydn's oratorio

of the "Creation" in an eminently worthy manner, with full orchestra and organ accompaniment—the solos being taken by Mrs. French, Miss Taws and Miss Taylor; Messrs. Cross, Dyer, Bird and Cooper; the vocal conductors were Benjamin Carr, Benjamin Cross and Thomas Loud, and the instrumental conductors P. Gilles, Charles F. Hupfeld and George Klemm. The same oratorio was repeated successfully on the 2d of November following. So early in its history as June of this year the Society was called upon to relieve the necessities of a fellow-member, an organist of one of our oldest churches, and the sum of two hundred dollars was appropriated to his relief; and he was buried, and a modest monument erected to his memory, in St. Peter's church-yard, at the expense of the Society.

As larger accommodations were required, in 1824 a lot of ground was purchased for $7500, situate on Locust Street between Eighth and Ninth Streets, on which stood a church edifice, formerly occupied by a congregation under the pastoral charge of Rev. Thomas H. Skinner. The corner-stone of the new hall was laid May 25, 1824, and the building completed December 24 of that year, under the plan and superintendence of William Strickland, one of the members of the Society. The whole cost was as follows:

Cost of lot, ...	.	$7,500 00
" building, ...	.	12,968 56
Furniture, ...	.	2,219 51
Incidental expenses, . . .	.	859 01

$$\text{\$23,547 08}$$

In May the thanks of the Society were voted to the vestry of St. Stephen's Church, for their liberality in promoting the objects of the Society, by allowing the gratuitous use of the church building for the performance of Haydn's oratorio of the "Creation."

In May, 1825, steps were taken towards the formation of a school or Academy of Music, for promoting a more general knowledge of music and supplying the orchestra of the Society with skillful performers. In September the Academy was formally opened, under a corps of competent teachers, with twenty-five pupils. The Academy existed for six years, when, finding that its continuance entailed serious loss to the Society, it was closed.

November 10, 1826, was given the twelfth concert of the Society, in which the Misses Gillingham and Mr. Paddon took the principal parts. In this year it was proposed to establish the "American Journal of Fine Arts," to be conducted by a joint committee of the Pennsylvania Academy of the Fine Arts and the Musical Fund Society of Philadelphia.

The committee, to which the matter was referred, were wisely charged to make no arrangement that did not provide a reasonable assurance that the publication should not infringe upon the funds of the respective institutions. The project, however, was abandoned as not at that time practicable.

The great musical event of the following year was the appearance of Madame Malibran, usually styled *Signorina*, in a miscellaneous concert in the Musical Fund Hall.

The programme was as follows:

June 16, 1827. "First appearance of *Madame Malibran* in Philadelphia."

PART I.

Overture, ...	*Mozart.*
Aria—"Che farà,"	*Signorina.*
Aria—"Batti, batti,"	*Signorina.*
Accompanied by Mr. Gilles on the violoncello.	
"Home, Sweet Home,"	*Signorina.*
Minuetto, ...	*Haydn.*

PART II.

Overture, ...	*Haydn.*
Song—"The Light Guitar,"	*Signorina.*
Solo, violoncello, accompanied by . . .	*Signorina.*
"Nel cor più non mi sento," with variations, by .	*Signorina.*
"Di tanti palpiti,"	*Signorina.*

Leader—Mr. Hupfeld.   Piano—Mr. Da Coninck.

Admission, $2.

Her second concert was given at the new Chestnut Street Theatre, on Saturday evening, June 23, 1827.

April 30, 1828. The Society gave its sixteenth concert, presenting Handel's oratorio of the "Messiah," the solos being taken by Miss George, Master Mercer, and Messrs. Pearson, Cross, Horn and Bird.

December 11, 1828. The Society gave its seventeenth concert in aid of its funds. A solo and chorus from "Orpheus," and selections, vocal and instrumental, from Rossini, Mozart, Boieldieu, Mehul, Beethoven and Weber, made up the programme.

In 1829 a committee was appointed to ascertain and determine a standard concert-pitch. In the concerts of this year appeared the favorite singer James Howard, who lived in this city till his death, in 1848.

The twentieth concert took place November 26, 1829, the principal vocalists being Mr. and Mrs. Pearman, Mrs. Franklin and Mrs. Andrews; and Mr. Schindœlecker, violoncello.

The hall of the Society very soon became noted for its admirable acoustic qualities, being also well lighted, well ventilated, and sufficiently spacious to meet the demands of the community. Madame Malibran again appeared upon its stage in 1831, and was supported by the Italian basso Signor Montressor, one of the opera troupe of which she was the soprano. Mrs. Austin, an English lady, followed.

March 24, 1831. The Society gave its twenty-third concert, the vocal parts being sustained by Mme. Brichta and Mr. Milon; and the instrumental parts by Mr. Cuddy, flutist, and Mr. Norton, trumpeter; under the leadership of Mr. Hupfeld.

January 13, 1832. The twenty-fifth concert embraced the following talent: Mrs. Austin, Mr. Sinclair, Miss Sterling, Messrs. Reinhart and Schindœlecker.

The Society lost two of its most worthy members, Benjamin Cross and George Schetky, who were associated with the Society from its commencement. They devoted to it their time, talents and professional skill, and did much to foster a musical taste in the city.

March 7, 1833. The oratorio of "Moses in Egypt" was rendered, with the following effective cast:

Fornasari,	*Pharaoh.*
Corsetti,	*Moses.*
Pedrotti,	*Aaron.*
Signora Pedrotti,	*Esther.*
Signora Saccomini,	*Nicaule.*

November 28, 1833. A concert was given by the Society, in which appeared Mrs. Austin, Mr. Clussman, clarionet; Mr. H. J. Trust, on the harp; and Mr. Power, the Irish comedian.

In this year also appeared Mr. and Mrs. Wood,

who became established favorites, and whose popularity continued for a long time.

February 26, 1834. The Society gave its thirty-first concert, in which Mr. and Mrs. Wood and Mr. Taylor, pianist, took part.

The Society, in order to encourage original composition, offered prizes of silver goblets and gold medals for the best instrumental music for full orchestra, as well as for the best vocal piece. Somewhat later (April 2, 1839) a gold medal was awarded to M. Bagiola for the best instrumental piece for full orchestra.

October 8. Mr. Norton, who was trumpeter to the First City Troop of Philadelphia, gave a concert, at which Miss Watson made her first appearance; Mrs. Franklin and Mr. Archer assisted.

In 1835 the hall was engaged for several purposes. The Society presented the oratorio of the "Seasons;" Miss Watson, Mr. Hupfeld, Mr. Hanna, Mr. Knight, Mr. Dempster, the ballad singer, appeared in concert; Horace Binney delivered an oration on the death of Chief Justice Marshall; Sheridan Knowles, the dramatist, Perdicaris, the Greek, and Dr. McMurtrie, Professor in the High School, lectured to large audiences; Mons. Adrian, the magician, also engaged the hall for his amusing performances.

November 26. The Society gave its first regular

concert of the season, with the assistance of Mrs. and Miss Watson and Signor Fabj in the vocal department, and Signor Krakamp and Mr. Shubert in the instrumental.

The Philharmonic Society—an organization composed of amateurs, led by a professional musician—gave its concerts in the Musical Fund Hall, which were of such excellence that it was thought by many that they were equal to those given by the Musical Fund Society. The societies, however, having different aims and purposes, ever acted in perfect harmony with each other, and it was not uncommon to find the subscribers to the one members of the other. The Philharmonic Society ceased to exist several years ago.

May 4, 1836. Mr. and Mrs. Wood, Brough and Walton appeared in the first part of " La Sonnambula," with the chorus and orchestra of the Chestnut Street Theatre. Mrs. Wood, in the rôle of *Amina*, had achieved a great reputation, which she fully merited. October 12, Signors Gambati, Cioffi, Fabj and Madame Otto appeared in a grand concert. Signor Cioffi performed on the trombone, an instrument then so little known and appreciated that, at the time of the organization of the Society, there was not one to be found in Philadelphia, and the loan of one was sought for in Bethlehem, fifty miles dis-

2

tant. Signor Gambati and John T. Norton competed for the public favor upon the trumpet, the former using the valve and the latter the plain trumpet. Miss Minna Overstoltz, a German pianist, displayed great proficiency in the performance of a rather limited repertoire; she appeared in the Society's first concert of the season, December 8, together with Miss Watson, Mr. and Mrs. Morley and Mr. Gilles, violoncellist, the orchestra being under the direction of Mr. Hupfeld.

On December 31, David Paul Brown delivered a eulogy on William Rawle, an esteemed and distinguished member of the Philadelphia bar.

1837. January 18, Mr. Charles Seitz, from Vienna, gave a grand concert, supported by Messrs. Keyser, Meignen, Peile, A. Schmitz, Hüttner, Cross and Seitz, instrumentalists, and the Misses Watson and Charlotte Ford, vocalists.

February 7. Mrs. Gibbs (formerly Miss Gradden), from England, appeared in the Society's regular concert; Mr. Charles F. Hupfeld, leader.

Mr. Hupfeld was one of the founders of the Society, and the first leader of its orchestra. He was born in Germany in 1787, arrived in this country at the age of fourteen, and died in this city July 15, 1864. He was an ornament to his profession, in which he filled a conspicuous part, and was greatly esteemed by all who knew him. He was created an honorary member of the Society in 1857.

The following is extracted from the Minutes of the Society :

"Mr. Hupfeld was the friend and associate of Benjamin Carr, George Schetky, P. Gilles, and his father-in-law, J. C. Homman, all names eminent in the musical circles of the day. These gentlemen and their younger colleagues, B. Cross, Joseph Taws and Thomas Loud, constituted the principal professional force, which, combined with the scientific and business aid of those lovers of music, the late Dr. Dewees and Dr. Patterson, Francis Gurney Smith and John K. Kane, founded the Musical Fund Society at a period when music, if not in its infancy in this country, was very far from being what it has since become, and which owes much of its present elevation to the exertions of these gentlemen, and to the organization of which they were the founders."

The third concert of the season was given May 12, on which occasion the Society secured the assistance of Signora Rossi, Signor Valtellina, primo basso cantante of the Havana Italian Company, and Signor Natale Felice.

A concert was given in the hall, October 13, by Signor Paggi, who performed on the oboe, assisted by Signora Ruiz-Garcia, the sister of the late Mme.

Malibran, Miss Charlotte Ford, Signor Valtellina, basso, and Signor Rapetti, violinist.

October 20, the Prague Company of Nine Professors of Music gave their farewell concert.

Gas was first introduced into the hall September 26, 1837, and greatly added to the brilliancy of the evening entertainments.

In November the Constitutional Convention to reform the Constitution of the State met in the hall, and held its sessions there for the ensuing ninety days.

In 1838, March 12, appeared Mme. Caradori-Allen, an English singer of rare excellence, who won "golden opinions" from an enthusiastic public; Brough, basso; De Begnis, buffo; Fornisari, of the Italian opera; and later in the year Henry Russell, the English baritone, whose songs became universally popular. "Silk" Buckingham delivered a course of agreeable lectures on Oriental travel, in a somewhat conversational style and in a sitting posture, then quite new to our audiences.

The Society gave its first concert of the season, the forty-fourth, November 15, the principal performers being Mme. Caradori-Allen, Henry Russell, Mr. Pfaff and Mr. A. Reinhart. Mr. Reinhart led the orchestra and Mr. Jarvis presided at the pianoforte.

Haydn's oratorio of the "Seasons" was given,

February 25, 1839, as the forty-fifth concert of the Society, and repeated shortly afterward. It was regarded as the great musical performance of the year.

In the same year Signor Fabj, Dempster, the Scotch ballad-singer, Mr. Wilson and Miss Shireff, often appeared in concert, and all became great favorites with the public. Professor George Combe delivered a course of lectures on Phrenology; Miss Pardi, a pupil of the harpist Bochsa, gave a concert on the 1st of October, and John T. Norton on the 30th of the same month. December 5, the Society gave its first concert of the season, the forty-sixth, when Mr. and Mrs. Seguin sang, Miss Pardi played on the harp, and Signor Ribas on the oboe. The orchestra was led by Mr. Reinhart, and the principal parts were sustained by Hupfeld, Keyser, Gambati, Meignen, Fiot, Hüttner, Rasché, B. C. Cross, Piele, Frederick, Carr, Jarvis, Reinstein, Riman, T. Cross, Worrall and Blanchor.

In 1840, January 23, was rendered Neukomm's oratorio of "David;" and later Braham, the English tenor, then a very old man, gave a concert of sacred music, in which he sang selections from Handel, and Luther's grand hymn, "Great God, what do I see and hear!" He was assisted by Mrs. Edward Loder, Mr. and Mrs. C. E. Horn. Concerts were given by an English troupe, comprising, among others, Signor

Giubelei, Miss Poole and Mr. Manvers. Kossowski, a Polish pianist, Mr. and Mrs. Watson appeared in concerts, and the Rev. Dr. Moriarty lectured.

A. Romberg's "Song of the Bell" was rendered, November 5, in the forty-ninth concert of the Society. Though brought out with much spirit, it was, in a pecuniary point of view, a failure, entailing a loss to the Society of about five hundred dollars. Two other concerts followed, which were also attended with pecuniary loss.

February 8, 1841. Through the exertions and under the management of Mr. William Norris, Jr., there was presented the "Zauberflöte," the "Magic Flute," in which Mme. Otto, Miss Poole, Messrs. Manvers, Seguin, Giubelei and Lasham, took the principal parts.

The concerts then given were mostly instrumental. Dona Dolores Nevares de Goni, guitarist, gave very entertaining performances, as also did the handsome Nagel, from Stockholm, a pupil of Paganini. Knoop, the violoncellist, Hervig, the violinist, and Miss Slomans, the pianist, also gave successful concerts.

In 1842 the Rev. John Newlin Maffitt, an eloquent but eccentric Methodist preacher, delivered a series of lectures; the Rainer family gave concerts; Signor Ribas performed solos on the oboe, and Max Bohrer on the violoncello.

The Rainers were five in number; they appeared in the costume of the Tyrol, and sang their national melodies with great effect.

In 1843 there appeared in the hall, successively, the Seguins, Mr. Bley, violinist; Professors Wines and Greenback, lecturers; Nourrit, Professor of vocal music in the Conservatoire of Paris; W. Vincent Wallace, the composer of "Maritana"; Signora Castellan, the Havana troupe, Madame Cinti Dammerau, and Artot, the distinguished violinist.

December 14, at the fifty-seventh concert, appeared Mme. Castellan and Signor Giampietro.

Ole Bull, the Norwegian violinist, gave a concert on December 16.

In 1844 came the Hutchinsons from the "Old Granite State"; a family, sixteen in number, familiarly known as "The Tribe of Jesse." Asa B. Hutchinson, who composed many of their most successful songs, and who was the youngest of the brothers, died very recently (Nov. 25, 1884), leaving but two members of the family surviving, John and Abby.

Signor Casella, violoncellist to the King of Sardinia, gave a concert; Professor Felix Gouraud gave lectures on Mnemotechny, or the Art of Memory, by which dates, or any combination of figures, could be remembered at the moment with the greatest ease;

Vieuxtemps, the famous violinist, chevalier of several orders, gave his first concert in the hall.

It was during the performance of that evening, May 4, 1844, occurred the commencement of the Kensington riots, which filled the whole city with alarm, and which finally resulted in the loss of human life and the destruction of valuable property.

The Swiss Bell Ringers, or Campanologians, a company composed of eight young men, appeared in September; and Henry Phillips, primo basso cantante of Her Majesty's concerts, made his first appearance in Philadelphia. His farewell concert was given December 6, 1844.

On the 11th of April the Society gave its fifty-eighth concert, in which they secured the services of Signorina Euphrasia Borghese, prima donna, and Signor Luigi Perozzi, primo tenore, of the Italian Opera. Signor Casella, violoncellist, also took part.

Ole Bull contributed his services without compensation at its fifty-ninth concert, Nov. 9, 1844, whereupon the Society presented to him, as a testimonial of its gratitude, a medal of pure gold, with suitable emblems and inscriptions, and constituted him an honorary member of the Society.

Loewe's oratorio of "The Seven Sleepers," founded on an interesting legend of the early days of Christianity, was rendered by the Sacred Musical Society,

December 26, in the hall of the Musical Fund Society. The vocal parts were taken by Miss Barry, Mrs. Taylor, Mr. Barclay, Mr. Jacobs, Mr. J. M. Bird and others; and the instrumental by Messrs. Meignen, Cross, Reinhart, Rudolph, Stolte, L. Rink, Hædrich, Wieland, H. Beck, Kellner, Elder, Stoll, F. Rink, Stevenson and others. This concert was repeated March 25 of the following year, and Miss Barry, a lady of distinguished musical abilities, took part on both occasions.

January 28, 1845. The Society's concert, the sixtieth, introduced Signora Pico, her first appearance; Signors Antognini and Sanquirico were also engaged. In the next concert of the Society, April 17, was given a grand military sinfonia, entitled "The Soldier's Dream," by Leopold Meignen, which was received with much favor as the production of an esteemed townsman.

June 20 was brought out the opera of "Leonora," by Wm. H. Fry, another gifted townsman. The opera was given with a grand chorus of seventy ladies and gentlemen, and an orchestra of fifty instruments, under the leadership of Leopold Meignen. Its rendition may be regarded as the musical event of the year. The composer was ambitious that it should be successful, and no expense was spared to make it so. Notwithstanding this and the engagement of the best available talent, the result, upon the whole, was a disappointment.

Professor Horncastle gave a concert in September, and the "Fakir of Ava," with his legerdemain performances, occupied the hall for one week. Faber's wonderful automaton was exhibited for a week in December, and Mr. Templeton, a Scotch tenor, gave his first concert immediately after. As a ballad-singer he was greatly admired.

During this season the orchestra of the Society performed very creditably the entire Symphony of Beethoven, No. 1, C major, which is ranked as one of the noblest of musical compositions. Eugene Provost, a musician of considerable ability, played a descriptive overture of the battle of New Orleans.

1846. Leopold De Meyer, a celebrated pianist, gave a few concerts, assisted by Joseph Burke, better remembered as "Master Burke," the youthful Roscius of the stage, who first appeared at the Arch Street Theatre Dec. 14, 1830. As a violinist he was regarded as but a mediocre performer, and failed utterly to enkindle the enthusiasm which greeted his early performances as an actor. Henri Herz followed De Meyer. The styles of these two distinguished pianists were in strong contrast, and represented two opposite schools. A very remarkable violinist now appeared, and one who is still remembered as the greatest of his day, Camillo Sivori. In a concert given by him, Dec. 10, he was assisted by F. Rudolph, H. Thorbecke, Miss Julia L. Northall and Signor De Begnis.

December 22. The Society gave a concert, engaging Signora Pico and Herz.

April 6, 1847. The Society gave its sixty-fifth concert, assisted by ladies and gentlemen amateurs of the city. This was the last concert given in the hall prior to important improvements. The front of the building was extended sixteen feet, and the position of the stage removed from the front to the rear. These changes happily improved the acoustics of the auditorium, and gave additional accommodations to the Society. The hall was enabled now to seat 1500 persons comfortably. The expenses of these alterations were mostly provided for by the proceeds of a grand bazaar fair, conducted by the leading ladies of society in the city. The fair continued a fortnight and realized about $5000, a sum which almost equalled the cost of the improvements. These improvements were commenced June 17, and finished on the 21st of October following. The bazaar ball was one of the great events of the season, and was for a long time the town-talk.

1847. Henry Giles, a Unitarian minister of marked critical ability, delivered a popular course of lectures on characters of Shakespeare. Signor Noronha appeared in concert. Samuel Lover, the author of "Handy Andy" and other Irish novels, novelist, song-writer and vocalist, made his first appearance.

December 11. Bochsa, the greatest harpist that had ever been heard in America, gave a concert in which Madame Anna Bishop sang.

January 1, 1848. In the farewell concert given by Madame Anna Bishop, she sang in costume a grand scena from "Tancredi" and "Guadalquivir." She was esteemed a good artist, possessing a high soprano voice. She was the wife of Sir Henry Bishop, a distinguished musical composer. Her fine soprano voice was cultivated, it is said, by Bochsa. Her first appearance in public was in London, in 1839, at a concert given by Bochsa, in which she shone brightly amidst a galaxy of celebrities consisting of Grisi, Pauline Viardot-Garcia, Persiani, Rubini, Tamburini and Lablache. All sang on this occasion. Thalberg and Dobler presided at the piano, and Bochsa at the harp.

February 2. The Steyermarkische Orchestra appeared at the hall, under the leadership of Riha.

February 3. The Society gave its sixty-sixth concert. The orchestra presented Mozart's overture to "Il Flauto Magico," and Lindpaintner's overture to the lyrical drama of "Lichtenstein." The vocal parts were sustained by a number of ladies and gentlemen amateurs. Mr. Edward L. Walker, pianist, made his first appearance as a member of the Society.

March 25, took place the farewell concert of the Italian Opera Company, in which appeared Signori Beneventano, Rossi, Corsi, Benedetti, Avignone, Bellini and Sanquirico, the buffo cantato; Signorina Truffi, Amalia Patti, Signora Biscaccianti and Lietti Corsi.

April 3, was rendered the sixty-seventh concert of the Society, in which were engaged Biscaccianti, Signor T. Vietti, Novello and Halma. Signora Biscaccianti, *née* Ostrinelli, was born in America, and made her debut in Philadelphia, March 1, in "Lucia de Lammermoor." She possessed a clear soprano voice, with excellent execution. Signor Novelli had a rich, deep bass, round and full.

May 25. The Society gave its sixty-eighth concert. On this occasion Rossini's "Stabat Mater" was performed, the vocal parts being sustained by Signor Perelli, first tenor of the Havana Opera Company, and Signor Avignone, first baritone of the Astor Place Opera Company, New York; together with the amateur members of the Society.

October 7. The Italian Opera gave a brilliant concert, in which appeared Signorina Amalia Patti, Benedetti, Debreul, Arnoldi, Rosi, Valtellina and Giubelei. A portion of the members of the Society assisted, and the whole comprised an orchestra of sixty performers and a chorus of fifty voices.

August 19. In concert appeared Arditi, violinist, and Bottesini, a remarkable performer on the contrabasso.

October 17. At the sixty-ninth concert appeared Mme. and Mons. Laborde, of the Royal Opera, Brussels, and Maurice Strakosch, pianist to the Emperor of Russia.

On December 3, 1848, was given the first concert of the Germania Musical Society, from Berlin. This organization was composed of twenty-three performers, under the leadership of Carl Lenshow. Four consecutive concerts were given in the hall, which, unfortunately, were not successful. The pecuniary losses attending these concerts determined the members to disband. Some went to New York, others to Boston and Baltimore, and one entered the United States military service as bandmaster. Of the original orchestra we note as still resident among us Mr. Carl Sentz, whose reputation as a musical director is so well known, and Mr. Carl Plagemann, the "first horn."

The Society was reorganized under the leadership of Carl Bergmann, and for many years subsequently gave a series of popular concerts in the hall.

1849 proved an interesting year in the musical

history of the Society. Maretzek, on the 4th of January, gave a grand festival, introducing all the artists of his popular troupe, Mme. Laborde, M. Laborde, Signor Sanquirico, Mr. Kyle, on the flute, Herr Lecroix, Herr Schreiver, Signorina Patti, Signor Novelli, Signor Dage, Herr Wind, Signor Mochi, with the opera orchestra and the Saxonia band, to which was added a part of the orchestra of the Society. The whole was under the direction of Max Maretzek. The trumpets were led by Herr Wind and Herr Lecroix; violins, viola and violoncello, by Herr Schreiver, Simonson, Hegeland and Eichorn.

February 9, the Society gave its seventieth concert, having engaged the talent of Mme. Anna Bishop, Signor Natale Perelli, Bochsa, harpist, Diston and his three sons, the celebrated performers on the silver Sax-horns and Sax-tubas.

March 14, Josef Gung'l, the composer, introduced his famous orchestra of twenty-six performers. In a vocal concert, given April 10, Tedesco, Rosina Pico, Vietti (C. and T.), appeared. Tedesco at once was declared a prime favorite. Madame Laborde achieved her laurels in Donizetti's opera of " L'Elisire d'Amore," and appeared in the Society's seventy-first concert, May 24, together with Valentini, Taffanelli and Carl Hohnstock.

October 15. In the seventy-second concert appeared Madame Amanda Berton, prima donna; Mons. Berton and Signor Vita, of the Havana Company; Luigi and Anniball Elena, violin and piano.

Beginning November 24, there were given several amateur musical soirees, conducted by ladies and gentlemen amateurs, with a full orchestra under the direction of Sig. Natale Perelli.

December 8. Musical Fund Society's seventy-third concert. Truffi, Carranti Vita, Benedetti, Vita and Rosi. Signora Truffi and Signor Benedetti were ever received with fervent applause, if not with *furore*, and maintained to the end their popularity. After many engagements together in public life, they entered into a more private engagement of their own, and were soon after happily married.

Many will recall with pleasure the estimable Hohnstocks, Carl and Adele, brother and sister, who made their home in this city. By their private instruction on violin and piano, and chamber concerts, they contributed much to the cultivation of a pure and refined musical taste.

In this year (May, 1849) the Society lost one of its oldest members, Benjamin Carr, who for a long time performed in the orchestra. By a strange coincidence, on the same day and nearly at the same hour, his wife also died. They had passed their lives together, and in death were not divided. They were buried in the same grave and at the same time. His portrait is preserved in the hall of the Society.

May 30, 1850. The Society gave its seventy-fourth concert, conducted by L. Meignen. The orchestra performed Mendelssohn's "Midsummer Night's Dream" and Weber's "Euryanthe." The vocal parts were rendered by Madame Bertucca, Miss Caroline Pintard, Signor Beneventano, baritone, and Master Diez.

September 3 was eventful in that the illuminating gas used in the city by some accident went out, leaving the city in comparative darkness, and inflicting much discomfort on the crowds gathered in our places of public amusement.

During this year Jenny Lind, the "Swedish Night-ingale," arrived, and gave her first concert at the Chestnut Street Theatre. Her terms were $1000 per night and all expenses paid. On account of the smallness of the theatre, her next two concerts were given at the Musical Fund Hall, October 18 and 19, 1850, realizing nearly nineteen thousand dollars; and other concerts followed, November 27, 29 and 30. Her last concerts took place in the same hall, December 16, 19 and 22. She generously contributed $400 to the funds of the Society, for which she received a resolution of thanks, and her name was enrolled among its honorary members. Natale

3

Perelli accompanied her as principal tenor. He made Philadelphia his home from that time till his death, in 1867, giving instruction in vocal music to a large number of pupils. An artistic monument erected to his memory in ~~Laurel Hill Cemetery~~ attests the respect of his many friends and admirers.

January 1, 1851. Theresa Parodi gave a festival concert, assisted by Mlle. Amalia Patti, Signors Lorini, Rosi and Avignone. The violinist, Herr Griebel, made his first appearance in Philadelphia. The orchestra was composed of fifty instruments.

April 24 was given the seventy-sixth concert of the Society, at which appeared Signora Angiolina Bosio, Signor Bettini, Signor Cesare Badiali, all members of the Havana Italian Opera Company; and Koppitz, flutist.

September 25. Mlle. Parodi gave another concert, supported by Amalia Patti, Strakosch, Leonardi and Master Charles M. Schmitz, the youthful violoncellist; Maurice Strakosch, conductor.

Miss Catharine Hayes, a singer of exquisite taste and feeling, appeared in concert Dec. 6 of the same year.

Mention should here be made of the Havana Italian Opera Troupe, which was composed of the following distinguished artistes, under the direction of F. Badiali: Signorina Balbina Steffanoni, Eliza

Costini, Signora L. Bellini, Signorina Bosio, Signora
C. Vietti, Sig. Domenico Lorini, F. Badiali, Ignazio
Marini, Colletti, T. Baritini, L. Martinelli, Serverro
Strini, P. Condi.

October 21, 1851. The Committee of Music reported adversely to the giving of the usual three concerts, and the Board accordingly ordered their sus-
pension. The minutes show that the deficiency or
loss sustained by the Society for the past five seasons,
in which were given fifteen concerts, amounted to
$1669.91. It was with great deliberation the Board
decided to give up its annual concerts, as the following extract most conclusively shows:

" If the past does not exhibit a fortunate result for
the interests of the Society, the future is still more
gloomy in prospect if the concerts be persisted in.
The increased and increasing demands of the fre-
quenters of musical entertainments cannot be satisfied
with anything less than the leading artists of the
time ; and the cost of engaging such talent is so great
that the Society cannot be indemnified at the present
scale of prices. The charter of the Society declares
two essential objects for which the corporation was
created, one of which is the cultivation of skill and
the diffusion of taste in music. At the date of the
Society's birth, and for many years thereafter, this
object was efficiently carried out by the concerts and

musical performances of its professional members. It took the lead in musical art, and did much in forming and encouraging a fondness for and correct taste in music. But its usefulness and power in this particular have been superseded. The sources are so numerous and the competition so full in the department of music that the Society can no longer produce entertainments to vie with those of others, and its concerts must necessarily be inferior to those undertaken by private enterprise.

"It has been thought by some that an obligation to the life-members of the Society requires that a certain number of concerts shall be regularly given. Such a conclusion is not founded on any article in either the Charter or the By-laws.

"It is not believed that our life-members, after being made acquainted with the situation of affairs and the unavoidable losses attendant on the concerts, would wish to listen to entertainments which greatly diminish the prospect of fulfilling the chief purpose of the foundation, namely, 'the relief of decayed musicians and their families'; nor will they, we feel confident, claim that funds so sacred in their creation and object should be squandered for their amusement."

1852. June 3. Parodi gave her last concert in America, assisted by Amalia and Maurice Strakosch, and Miska Hauser, violinist.

September 21. Signorina Adelina Patti, not yet eight years old, styled "*la petite* Jenny Lind," appeared in concerts, with the support of the Strakoschs and Miska Hauser.

September 27. Mme. Marietta Alboni appeared.

October 14. Mme. Henrietta Sontag (Countess Rossi) made her first appearance, supported by Sig. Badiali, Paul Julien, violin, Alfred Jaell, piano, and the Germania Musical Society. Her last appearance in the hall was on the evening of November 26. This beautiful woman and delightful singer died in Mexico, June 18, 1864, under the saddest circumstances, deeply regretted by an admiring, music-loving public.

Upon the engagement of Mme. Sontag to sing, a delegation of the Musical Fund Society met her on her arrival at the wharf at Burlington, N. J., on the Delaware river, and escorted her to this city. Mr. George Campbell, the Secretary of the Society, made an address of welcome, which was gracefully responded to by Mme. Sontag. Refreshments had been amply provided on board the steamboat; and the music was rendered by the Germania Orchestra. Badiali, Rocco (buffo), Paul Julien and Alfred Jaell took important parts in the programme. The reception was such as to call forth the most enthusiastic acknowledgments by the fair songstress. She was afterward elected an honorary member of the Society.

December 3.   The Society gave its seventy-eighth concert.   The overtures were Rossini's "Otello" and Weber's "Obéron."   Mlle. Mina Tourny, mezzo-soprano, Mlle. Louisa Tourny, contralto, Mlle. Camille Urso, violinist, Signor Giuseppe Cortesi, tenor, and Signor Giuseppe Foghel, violinist, filled up the programme.

December 11.   A concert was given by Mme. Henrietta Sontag, for the benefit of the Society, in which she was assisted by the following artistes of her company: Signor G. Pozzolini, Signor Rocco and Paul Julien.

Madame Stephani appeared also about this time, and the English basso, John Graham.   Lectures were delivered by Elihu Burritt, "the learned blacksmith," and Park Benjamin, the journalist.

1853.   Lectures were given in the hall by the novelist, William Makepeace Thackeray, and Father Gavazzi, the Italian reformer.   L. Moreau Gottschalk, the pianist, made his debut March 1.   He was born in New Orleans in 1828, and his musical career in the United States was highly prosperous.   His compositions enjoyed for a long period a remarkable popularity.

June 26 appeared Augustus Braham, son of the

celebrated English tenor John Braham, whose original patronymic was Abraham.

May 15, 1854. Paul Julien, a violinist of exquisite taste, gave a concert, when again appeared the youthful Adelina Patti, who won all hearts by her winning ways and her birdlike voice, giving promise of the distinguished career which awaited her. She rapidly rose to be the leading soprano in Europe, and she sang in Philadelphia for the last time in the winter of 1884–5 with the greatest applause.

January 10, 1855. Under the management of Strakosch there appeared upon our lyric stage two vocalists whose reputation will never die, Madame Grisi and Signor Mario.

Felicita Vestvali, who was born in Cracow, Feb. 23, 1839, made her debut at the hall, September 29, 1855. She was a remarkable woman, speaking in six languages and playing upon several musical instruments. Her singing was appreciated by all lovers of music.

Miss Louisa Pyne, who, at the early age of five, exhibited extraordinary musical gifts, and had made a successful debut at a concert before she had completed her tenth year, formed an English opera company, together with Mr. William Harrison, and now appeared in concert.

June 6. Madame La Grange produced a deep and lasting impression by her rich and wonderful volume of voice and admirable vocalization.

The eighty-first concert of the Society was given the 29th of September, with the aid of the following artistes: Mlle. Vestvali, contralto; Signor Ceresa, tenor; Signor Bernardi, baritone, and Herr Schreiber, cornet player. The pecuniary loss attending this fine concert was $498.55. Not intimidated by this loss, the Society, Dec. 1, gave its eighty-second concert, in which appeared Miss Hensler, an American prima donna, her first appearance; Signorina Aldini, her first appearance; Signor Brignoli, from the Italian Opera, Paris, his second appearance in this city; and L. M. Gottschalk, pianist, assisted by the full orchestra of the Society, conducted by Leopold Meignen. The pecuniary loss by this concert was $456.84.

The expenses attending the concerts and oratorios given by the Society exhausted its resources, and it became apparent to the managers that every succeeding concert worthy of the Society must increase its embarrassment. The performers of any acknowledged reputation demanded the most extravagant rates of compensation, ranging between $100 and $500 a night; and only the most celebrated artistes could fill the hall. Under these circumstances money was borrowed upon bond and mortgage, to extricate the Society from its financial embarrassment, and to provide for the relief of its beneficiaries.

During the many years of its existence the Society has received, we believe, but a single legacy, and that for $1500, from Pierre Antoine Blenon, which was paid in installments in the years 1843 and 1844. Dr. John Rhea Barton, Sept. 28, 1847, made a donation of $100, and in 1851, Jenny Lind, as we have already stated, presented to the Society $400 in aid of its funds.

1856. The Society ordered to be painted the portraits of Dr. Wm. P. Dewees and Dr. Robert M. Patterson, former presidents; together with that of George Campbell, its late secretary, who for twenty-seven years had most faithfully performed all the duties of his office. Dr. Patterson was one of the founders of the Society, and one of its warmest, most steady and efficient supporters. He resigned only when, in 1853, his failing health had disabled him from watching over its interests.

April 10. The Society gave its eighty-third concert, in which appeared Madame Anna La Grange, Signor Brignoli and Signor Amodio; Perelli, piano. The loss by this concert was $183.35, making the total loss of $1138.74 as the result of these three concerts.

In September, 1856, an orchestra was formed in

this city consisting of twenty-eight professional members. As many of these members had been formerly connected with the Germania Musical Society, it was proposed to give to this organization the name of the *Germania Orchestra*, which it retains to this day, under the leadership of Charles M. Schmitz.

Their last public rehearsal was given May 4, 1868, at the Musical Fund Hall. A new series of rehearsals has been inaugurated, and continued to the present time, at the Academy of the Fine Arts.

The Orchestra gave their public rehearsals on Saturday afternoons in the hall, for many years, at very reduced prices of admission, — packages of eight tickets being sold for one dollar. While conferring great benefit and delight to the musical public, it is to be regretted that, in a pecuniary point of view, the concerts were productive of no profit to the Orchestra.

November 25. The eighty-fourth concert was given with very much the same leading voices; the aim of the Society being to maintain its high standard of music, though at the increasing risk of pecuniary loss.

April 25, 1857. The Society gave its eighty-fifth concert, at which appeared Madame Gazzaniga and Signori Brignoli and Arnoldi, supported by the full orchestra of the Society.

We pause in this sketch to throw a wreath upon the fresh grave of Signor Pasquale Brignoli, who died in the city of New York, October 30, 1884. He made his first appearance in Philadelphia, Jan. 14, 1856, in the opera of " Il Trovatore," in the Walnut Street Theatre, with Madame Anna La Grange, Mlle. Nantier Didiéé and Signor Amodio. He retained his beautiful tenor voice for more than thirty years, during which he sang with Parepa, La Grange, Piccolomini, Kellogg, Albani, Nilsson, Di Murska, Van Zandt, and all the great prime donne who have visited our shores. He made this country his place of residence, though for many years he was the leading tenor in London and Paris.

The advent of Madame Gazzaniga upon the lyric stage produced a marked sensation. She at once became an established favorite, and was the first soprano to inaugurate, on February 25, 1857, the opening of the new opera house—the American Academy of Music on Broad Street. Her marble bust graces the foyer of the building, placed there in honor of that occasion.

In April was brought out, under the auspices of the Society, the cantata of the " Cities of the Plain," composed by Mr. F. T. S. Darley, a member of the Society.

May 28. The eighty-sixth concert was given with

the aid of Madame Isidora Clark, Signori Brignoli and Amodio, and Herr Appy, harpist. This being the last concert given by the Society, we append the full programme as a reminiscence of the past.

MUSICAL FUND SOCIETY.

EIGHTY-SIXTH CONCERT.

Third of the Season, 1856–57.

The Managers of the MUSICAL FUND SOCIETY have the honor to announce that the

LAST CONCERT

of the season will be given at their hall, on

THURSDAY EVENING, MAY 28, 1857,

for which occasion they have engaged the following distinguished Artistes:

MADAME ISIDORA CLARK,

SIGNOR BRIGNOLI,

SIGNOR AMODIO, and

HERR HENRI APPY,

Solo Violinist to the King of Holland.

Assisted by the *Full Orchestra* of the Society.

L. MEIGNEN, *Conductor.*

Single Tickets, . . . *One Dollar each.*

Seats can be secured without extra charge, at the hall, on Tuesday, Wednesday and Thursday, from 9 A.M. to 6 P.M.

Carriages will set down heads east and take up heads west.

Doors open at 7. Concert to commence at 8 o'clock.

PROGRAMME.

PART FIRST.

1. Jubilee Overture, ... *C. M. Von Weber.*
   FULL ORCHESTRA.
2. Duo—"Ola bella immantimente,"—"Betly," . *Donizetti.*
   SIG. BRIGNOLI and SIG. AMODIO.
3. Gran Scena e Cavatina—"Anch'io dischiuso,"—
   Nabucco, ... *Verdi.*
   MADAME ISIDORA CLARK.
4. Aria—"Vieni la mia Vendetta,"—"Lucrezia Bor-
   gia," . . . . *Donizetti.*
   SIGNOR AMODIO.
5. *a.* Andante, } Second Grand Concerto, . *Mendelssohn.*
   b. Finale,
   HENRI APPY.
6. Romanza, ... *Lillo.*
   SIGNOR BRIGNOLI.
7. Cavatina—"The Lost Birdling," composed ex-
   pressly for Mme. Isidora Clark, . . . *Centemeri.*
   MADAME ISIDORA CLARK.

PART SECOND.

8. Overture—"The Merry Wives of Windsor" (first
   time in this city), ... *Otto Nicolai.*
   FULL ORCHESTRA.
9. Romanza—"A sperar non mai poss'io," . *M. De Gosio.*
   SIGNOR AMODIO.
10. Grand Waltz in Bravura, ... *Venzano.*
    MADAME ISIDORA CLARK.
11. Romanza—"La brezza allegia interno"—I Vespri
    Siciliani, ... *Verdi.*
    SIGNOR BRIGNOLI.

12. Il Tremolo—Grand Fantasia for Violin, . . *De Beriot.*
HENRI APPY.
13. Trio—"Attila," . . . . *Verdi.*
MADAME ISIDORA CLARK, SIG. BRIGNOLI and SIG. AMODIO.

September 25, 1857. A grand concert was given by Vieuxtemps, Thalberg, Mme. D'Angri and Rocco; and December 19 another grand concert was given by D'Angri and Vieuxtemps, assisted by Mlle. Carioli, Signors Labocetta and Gassen.

From this time the hall was mainly rented for lectures, assemblies, balls, parties and miscellaneous concerts. In these concerts frequently reappeared Elèna D'Angri, Thalberg, pianist and composer, Kopta and Vieuxtemps, violinists, and Parepa and other favorites, who rarely failed to fill the hall.

Among the lecturers we mention Rev. Henry Giles, Rev. Henry Ward Beecher, George W. Curtis, Edward Everett, Rev. Dr. Chapin and John B. Gough. Lectures were also given by Ralph Waldo Emerson, Rev. Dr. Tiffany, Bishop Stevens and "Adirondack" Murray, and at other times by Dr. Isaac Hayes, who had just returned from his Arctic expedition; George Francis Train, "Artemus Ward" Brown, and Edwin P. Whipple, the distinguished critic and essayist.

Lola Montez and Frezzolini appeared about this time. The latter gave a concert November 13. Frezzolini was a German soprano of some reputation in her day, and was the most popular opera singer in Paris. Her death has been reported as occurring quite lately, at the age of sixty.

The Society lost one of its oldest and most respected members—Mr. Benjamin Cross. He was born September 15, 1786, and received his musical education from Benjamin Carr. He was the organist in St. Mary's (Roman Catholic) Church in 1808. His first appearance as a public singer was in 1810, in an oratorio given at St. Augustine's (Roman Catholic) Church. He became one of the founders of the Musical Fund Society in 1820, and, together with Benjamin Carr and Thomas Loud, conducted the vocal department of the Society. He sang in the oratorio of the "Creation," June 10, 1822, given at Washington Hall; again at the opening of the Musical Fund Hall, in Locust Street, December 29, 1824, in Handel's "Dettingen Te Deum"; and in the oratorio of the "Messiah," performed April 30, 1828. He was elected a manager of the Society, May 2, 1820, and was ever a zealous member. He died March 1, 1857, in the seventy-first year of his age.

By resolution of the Board, the portraits of Judge John K. Kane and Benjamin Cross were painted by Thomas Sully for the Society. Judge Kane was one of the earliest and most ardent members of the

x his full name was

Society, and was one of the committee appointed to draft its constitution, in 1820. He first served as Secretary, then as Vice-president, and then as President.

In this year, also, the Board signified its appreciation of the faithful services of its Treasurer, Mr. Francis Gurney Smith, by ordering his portrait to be painted and placed among those of other founders and benefactors of the Society. Mr. Smith served the Society for forty-three years, carefully managing its funds and contributing largely to its success.

The opening of the Academy of Music virtually ended the public musical performances of the Musical Fund Society. Operas proved more attractive than concerts. Prime donne appeared to more advantage on the stage, with the accessories of costume and scenery, than upon the platform of the concert-room. And with this year began a new policy of the Society. Guided by the experience of the past, and influenced by the former action of the Board under similar circumstances, it was deemed expedient to discontinue the regular concerts of the Society, in order to carry out successfully one of its primary objects, namely, "the relief of decayed musicians and their families."

In the retrospect of this history of the Society, we believe that the labors of the managers for the cultivation of a pure taste and the diffusion of a greater love of music among all classes of the community have not been in vain. It may not be proper at this time to do more than allude to the beneficial operations of the Society in relieving its professional members and their families from the evils incident to poverty, sickness and old age. Many have been the prayers and grateful thanks of the widows and orphans who have been most liberally provided for under its sheltering arms. More than one hundred thousand dollars have been thus expended.

Since its organization the whole number of professional members reaches 149, and of amateur and honorary members 1171. At present the Society numbers 16 professional and 49 amateur members.

Mention should be made here of the long and faithful service of our late Superintendent, Mr. Thomas J. Beckett. Mr. Beckett became connected with the Society in 1834, and remained in office till 1880, when bodily infirmities and impaired health obliged him to decline a re-election. In accepting his resignation, the Board tendered to him the free use of the dwelling so long occupied by him, and passed the following complimentary resolutions :

"*Resolved*, That the Board of Directors of the Musical Fund Society, in accepting the resignation of Mr. Thomas J. Beckett as Superintendent of the

4

hall, expresses regret that failing health has compelled an old, faithful and much-respected servant to withdraw from that employment.

"For nearly one half century he has discharged his important trust with singular fidelity, always showing devotion to the best interests of the Society. The Board reluctantly accedes to the request of Mr. Beckett, and hopes that he may live to see many years of prosperity and happiness."

The future of the Society time alone can disclose. Its work is not yet done. We believe that it may yet be possible to repeat, under better auspices, the experiment made so unsuccessfully in its earlier history—namely, the establishment of an academy for instruction in vocal and instrumental music, with a corps of accomplished, competent and well-trained teachers. The further accumulation of funds for this object may be desired by the management, and this may in some respects decide its future policy. Meanwhile, care is exercised to protect and increase its funds, and, under the generous provisions of its by-laws, minister to its disabled professional members and their respective families.

LIST OF OFFICERS OF THE MUSICAL FUND SOCIETY.

PRESIDENTS.

William P. Dewees, M.D.,	1820 to 1838.
Robert M. Patterson, M.D.,	1838 " 1853.
Robley Dunglison, M.D.,	1853 " 1854.
John K. Kane,	1854 " 1856.
Robley Dunglison, M.D.,	1856 " 1869.
Franklin Peale,	1869 " 1870.
Richard J. Dunglison, M.D.,	1870.

VICE-PRESIDENTS.

Robert M. Patterson, M.D.,	1820 to 1829.
John K. Kane,	1829 " 1834.
William H. Keating, M.D.,	1834 " 1836.
Robert M. Patterson, M.D.,	1836 " 1838.
John K. Kane,	1838 " 1850.
Robley Dunglison, M.D.,	1850 " 1853.
Elkanah W. Keyser,	1853 " 1854.
Pierce Butler,	1854 " 1855.
Robley Dunglison, M.D.,	1855 " 1856.
Elkanah W. Keyser,	1856 " 1860.

Thomas Sully,	.	.	.	1860 to 1873.
Frederick A. Klemm,	.	.	.	1873 " 1876.
Charles F. Stolte, .	.	.	.	1876 " 1881.
William L. Mactier,	.	.	.	1881.

TREASURERS.

Daniel Lamont,	.	.	.	.	1820.
Francis Gurney Smith,	.	.	.	1820 to 1864.
William L. Mactier,	.	.	.	1864 " 1880.
Theodore Starr,	.	.	.	1880 " 1884.
John T. Jones,	.	.	.	1884.

SECRETARIES.

John K. Kane,	.	.	.	1820 to 1821.
William McIlhenny,	.	.	.	1821 " 1822.
Joseph W. Houston,	.	.	.	1822 " 1827.
George Campbell, .	.	.	.	1827 " 1856.
Louis C. Madeira, .	.	.	.	1856 " 1858.
William L. Dunglison, .	.	.	1858 " 1872.
James V. Patterson, M.D.,	.	.	1872.

LIST OF OIL PORTRAITS IN THE HALL OF THE MUSICAL FUND SOCIETY.

1. Benjamin Carr.
   > Painted by J. C. Darley, 1831.

2. George Schetky.
   > Painted by J. C. Darley.

3. Mrs. Julia Wood, as *Amina* in the opera of " La Sonnambula."
   > Painted by John Neagle, 1848, and presented by Dr. Joseph Togno.

4. George Campbell.
   > Painted by T. Sully, 1856.

5. Dr. William P. Dewees.
   > Painted by T. Sully, 1856.

6. Dr. Robert M. Patterson.
   > Painted by T. Sully, 1856.

7. Francis Gurney Smith.
   > Painted by T. Sully, 1857.

8. John K. Kane.
        Painted by T. Sully, 1861.

9. Benjamin Cross.
        Painted by T. Sully, 1861.

10. Thomas Sully.
        Painted by himself, 1867.

11. Dr. Robley Dunglison.
        Painted by T. Sully, 1868.

12. Franklin Peale.
        Painted by T. Sully, 1868.

The Officers and Directors of the Musical Fund Society, are respectfully invited to attend the funeral of

THOMAS J. BECKETT,

late Superintendent, from their Hall on Locust Street above Eighth, on Wednesday next, at 11 A. M.

THE
MUSICAL FUND
SOCIETY.

SOUVENIR OF OCTOBER 28, 1891.

Descriptive Souvenir

Commemorative of the Opening

OF THE

MUSICAL FUND HALL,

No. 808 LOCUST STREET,

PHILADELPHIA.

FOR THE SEASON OF 1891-1892.

Programme.

PART I

UNDER MR. SIMON HASSLER, CONDUCTOR.

1. Pas Redouble—"Eu Avant" . . . . *Gungl*
2. Overture—"La Gazza Ladra" . . . . *Rossini*
3. Grand Selection—"Aida" · . . . . *Verdi*
4. Intermezzo · · · · · · · · · · · · · · · · · · · *Delibes*
5. Larghetto—from Second Symphony · · · · · · *Beethoven*
6. Salterella · *Gounod*
7. Gavotte—"Hildegarde" · · · · · · · · · *Geo. P. Kimball*
8. Waltz—"Editorial" · · · · · · · · · · · · · *Johann Strauss*

PART II

UNDER MR. CHARLES M. SCHMITZ, CONDUCTOR.

9. Marche aux Flambeaux · · · · · · · · · · · · *Meyerbeer*
10. Loin du Bal · · · · · · · · · · · · · · · · · · · *Gillet*
11. Polka—"Gambrinus" · · · · · · · · · · · · · · · *Bial*
12. Grand Selection—"Der Freischutz" · · · *Von Weber*
13. Waltz—"Convent Echoes" · · · · · · · · · · · *Le Thiere*
14. Selection—"Lohengrin" · · · · · · · · · · · · *Wagner*
15. Polka—"Journalist" · · · · · · · · · · · · *Simon Hassler*
16. March—"Wedding" · · · · · · · · · · · · · · *Mendelssohn*

Announcement.

The Musical Fund Society, through its Building Committee, has thought the occasion of the re-opening of the Hall, with all its new decorations and advantages, for the Season of 1891-1892, to be a fitting opportunity to issue this Descriptive Souvenir, not only for the purpose of making a public announcement, but also to commemorate the event. The following description of the alterations and changes which have taken place during the past summer will, it is believed, be found interesting to the many friends of the Society, and at the same time be acceptable as a souvenir of the evening.

The present improvements were first proposed to the Directors at a stated meeting held in January, 1891, and from that time the Board have been practically unanimous in the efforts to rejuvenate the property of the Society. The original proposition included the appointment of a "Building Committee" of five, who were authorized to secure the services of a competent architect, and with his assistance to construct or devise a plan and offer suggestions for such alterations and decorations as would carry into effect the ideas approved of by the Board of Directors, reporting the same at the following stated meeting. The Committee consisted of:

MR. GEORGE P. KIMBALL, *Chairman.*
DR. RICHARD J. DUNGLISON.
DR. CHARLES P. TURNER.
MR. WILLIAM HENRY LEX.
MR. MURRAY GIBSON.
MR. WILLIAM S. ROBINSON.

The Committee were most enthusiastic as to the purpose of their appointment and at once entered into a full consideration of the whole subject.

Mr. Addison Hutton, a gentleman too well and favorably known to all Philadelphians (and especially to those in his own profession) to need any complimentary remarks at this time, was selected as the Architect, and the Committee feel assured that the appointment was in every way a most judicious one.

Many meetings were held and many suggestions discussed, but finally a full set of plans—including needed alterations to the building, an annex and numerous other changes in regard to lighting, decorations, etc —were presented to the Directors at a meeting held in May.

The plans as presented and explained were at once approved and accepted, and full authority was given to the Building Committee to act in the matter. The Committee, through the architect, Mr. Hutton, received proposals from builders, artisans and others to do the work, the contracts of the following gentlemen or firms being accepted :

1. JACOB MYERS, No. 1315 Sansom Street, for all alterations and annex building.
2. JOHN GIBSON, No. 123 South Eleventh Street, for all the painting and decorations. Mr. Murray Gibson representing the firm.
3. THE DE KOSENKO & HETHERINGTON MANUFACTURING COMPANY, No. 808 Sansom Street, for all the gas fixtures and electroliers.
4. THE NOVELTY ELECTRIC COMPANY, No. 50 North Fourth Street, for all wiring for electric lights and electric lighting of gas.

Attention is particularly called to the following changes in the building :

The Front.

The entire front of the Hall will be new ; a combination of buff brick, terra-cotta facings and copper cornices, having been most artistically used by the architect, the general result being a very bright and effective front, not only ornamental and dignified, but in excellent good taste, and with first-class wearing qualities. New windows have been made in the two office-rooms on the first floor. The steps at the main entrance, which formerly occupied one-half the pavement, have been set back, so that all but three of the steps are now within the front building line. This improvement is most useful on account of the increased facility for exit.

First Floor Corridor.

Upon entering the building, the first noticeable changes are the two entirely new stairways leading to the Main Saloon on the second floor. Formerly, as most of our patrons will remember, there were two flights to each stairway, as now, but the stairs of the second flight all converged to a point, giving, on account of this fault, only one-half use of the flight, besides making a most dangerous mode of exit. This, as will be seen, has been corrected, and now the second flight is of full width—each stair being the same—and the top landing on a level with the floor of the Main Saloon, doing away with the single odd step directly at the entrance door.

The centre partition and all the sides are finished in hard wood, and open brass grille-work has been used in completing the upper half of the partition—in this way giving ventilation and a greater diffusion of the light from one stairway to the other. The effect will be noticed by everyone.

Waiting-Room for Ladies,

This room, on the right of the entrance corridor, is 51 feet long and 22 feet wide. It has seating capacity for about two hundred (200) persons, and could be used for small meetings or entertainments. In the event of a Ball or Assembly it is used as a " Waiting-room for Ladies," and has all the requisite toilet conveniences for their welfare and comfort. A large wardrobe for wraps and clothing is connected with this room. The room has been entirely replastered, painted, decorated and furnished with new gas fixtures and electroliers.

_____

Waiting-Room for Gentlemen.

This room, on the left of the entrance corridor, is quite large and has a commodious wardrobe, for the storing of wraps and coats, connected with it, also toilet rooms, etc. In the event of a Ball, it can be used as a Gentleman's Refreshment-room. It has just been painted, decorated, and new gas fixtures introduced.

The Banquet Room.

At the extreme end of the entrance corridor is the Banquet-room, the second largest saloon, which has been lengthened about thirty (30) feet, mak-ing the saloon eighty-seven (87) feet long and thirty (30) feet wide, with a seating capacity for four hundred (400) persons. A small stage has been erected at the western end, with a private exit door for perform-ers. This saloon is an excellent one for small parlor con-certs, small entertainments, meetings. and for banquets, dinners and suppers. In the latter cases a regular kitchen, with complete range and cooking facilities, is directly connected with the saloon ; and this advantage, together with use of the " Waiting-room for Ladies " as a place for guests to assemble, makes a very complete suite of rooms for such entertainments. The room has been entirely painted and newly decorated, new gas fix-tures and electroliers being introduced.

_____

The Annex Building.

In considering the alterations and improvements, it was decided that an " Annex Building " on the adjoining premises (owned by the Society) would be an advantage. This idea has been carried into effect, and the result is a two-story brick building which not only gave thirty (30) feet additional length to the Banquet room, but enabled the architect to provide three Parlors or Reception-rooms on the second floor, en suite, and having direct connection with the Main Saloon. Two of these parlors are on a level with the floor of the Main Saloon ; the third is five feet higher, on a level with the floor of the stage. It is the intention to use this last described room as a private room for Prima Donnas, or leading artists, during performances, as direct entrance to the stage can be made from it, and the room has been furnished with this purpose in view. All the rooms have been newly furnished and decorated and will be found most attractive. These parlors are to be rented or not, with a rental of the Main Saloon. For an Assembly or Ball, the advantage of three such retiring rooms for conversation or rest will be appreciated by all.

The Main Saloon.

This Saloon, which has a world-wide reputation, has not been changed, so far as the formation of the room is concerned ; but it was thought a wise step to erect an entirely new stage, which should reach from wall to wall, the whole width of the Saloon, removing both partitioned rooms on each side of the old stage. This has been done and the stage has now seating capacity for about two hundred (200) persons. The seating capacity of the floor of the Main Saloon has also been increased to about twelve hundred (1200). The three large circular gas fixtures formerly hanging in the centre of the Saloon have been removed, the lighting now being made by a new arrangement from the side walls, a cluster of gas and electric lights being placed in semi-circular form over the top of each window. On the stage have been placed two large "Standards," each holding a cluster of gas and electric lights. The stage has also been provided with a full set of footlights in case they are needed.   The decorations of this Saloon are very beautiful, and Mr. Gibson, while his work in other parts of the building is in excellent good taste, has taken especial interest in the coloring and design of this room.   The general color is ivory with gilt and silver finish, and the effect is most happy.   About a year or so ago the entire floor of this Saloon was relaid with the best seasoned wood that could be obtained, great care being taken that it should be first-class in every way.

———

The Musical Fund Society feel much pleased at the result of their efforts, and are very confident that the improvements and advantages of the Hall will result in an increased desire for its use. Any one of its three Saloons—one with 2co seating capacity, another with 400, and still another for 12co— can be rented for any time of day or evening for Meetings, Concerts, Assemblies, Balls, Banquets, Dinners, Suppers, Fairs, or for small or large entertainments of different character.   There is a possibility that in the future a temporary frame work may be erected together with a curtain and a limited supply of scenery, so that private theatricals, tableaux and such performances may be given in the Hall.   It is hoped that a successful season will prove that the efforts of the Society to provide a first-class concert Hall are appreciated by the public.

History.

As many persons have not seen Mr. Wm. L. Mactier's sketch of The Musical Fund Society, published in 1885, it has been deemed advisable to insert here a few extracts from that interesting work :

"The Musical Fund Society of Philadelphia was "established February 29, 1820. It embraced professors "of music and amateur members. The first meeting "took place at Elliott's Hotel, Chestnut Street, January "7, 1820, Dr. Wm. P. Dewees in the chair, and John K. "Kane, Secretary.

    *   *   *   *   *

"The objects of the ʌ .ety were, first, to cultivate "and diffuse a musical taste ; and, secondly, to afford "relief to its necessitous pr ᷄   ional members and their "families. Its first conce᷄ was given on Tuesday, "April 24, 1821, at Washington Hall, Third Street above "Spruce Street. The orchestra and chorus consisted of "one hundred performers.

    *   *   *   *   *   *

"The most distinguished and estimable of our citi-"zens rapidly joined the Society, and became interested "in its advancement. Its first President was Dr. Wm. "P. Dewees, and its first Vice-President Dr. Robert M. "Patterson. Judge John K. Kane, Benjamin Say, "Francis Gurney Smith, Franklin Peale, Dr. R. "La Roche, Francis M. Drexel, Dr. George McClellan, "Thomas Sully, John Keating, Jr., William Meredith, "James Nebins, William Kneass, John F. Greland, Dr. "Isaac Hays, Abraham Ritter, and Francis Hopkinson. "became members in 1820.

    *   *   *   *   *   *

"As larger accommodations were required, in 1824 "a lot of ground was purchased for $7,500, situate on "Locust Street, between Eighth and Ninth Streets, on "which stood a church edifice, formerly occupied by a "congregation under the pastoral charge of Rev. Thos.

" H. Skinner. The corner-stone of the new Hall was
" laid May 25, 1824, and the building completed Decem-
" ber 24th, of that year, under the plan and superintend-
"ence of William Strickland, one of the members of
" the Society.
    *   *   *   *   *   *

" The Hall of the Society very soon became noted
" for its admirable acoustic qualities, being also well
" lighted, well ventilated, and sufficiently spacious to
" meet the demands of the community.
    *   *   *   *   *   *

" Gas was first introduced into the Hall, September
" 26, 1827, and greatly added to the brilliancy of the
" evening's entertainments.
    *   *   *   *   *   *

" In 1847 the front of the building was extended
" sixteen feet, and the position of the stage removed
"from the front to the rear. These changes happily
"improved the acoustics of the auditorium, and gave
" additional accommodations to the Society.
    *   *   *   *   *   *

" In 1857, the opening of the Academy of Music seri-
" ously affected the public musical performances of the
" Musical Fund Society. Operas proved more attractive
" than concerts. Prima donnas appeared to more advan-
" tage on the stage, with the accessories of costume and
"scenery, than upon the platform of the concert-room.
" And with this year began a new policy of the Society.
" Guided by the experience of the past, and influenced
" by the former action of the Board under similar cir-
" cumstances, it was deemed expedient to discontinue
" the regular concerts of the Society, in order to carry
" out successfully one of its primary objects, namely,
" ' the relief of decayed musicians and their families '
" In the retrospect of this history of the Society, we
" believe that the labors of the Managers for the culti-
" vation of a pure taste, and the diffusion of a greater
" love of music among all classes of the community,
" have not been in vain. It may not be proper, at this

"time to do more than allude to the beneficial oper-
"ations of the Society, in relieving its professional
"members and their families from the evils incident to
"poverty, sickness and old age. Many have been the
"prayers and grateful thanks of the widows and
"orphans who have been most liberally provided for
"under its sheltering arms. More than one hundred
"thousand dollars ($100,000) have been thus expended."

*   *   *   *   *   *

Between April 24, 1821, and May 28, 1857, eighty-
six (86) public concerts were given by the Musical Fund
Society. Many celebrated artists, both vocalists and
instrumentalists, appeared at these concerts. Among
them might be named :

Vocalists.

Mad Malibran	June 16, 1827
Mme. Brichta	Mar. 24, 1831
Signora Pedrotti	Mar. 7, 1833
Mrs. Austin	Jan'y 13, 1832
Mrs. Wood	Feb. 26, 1834
Mad. Otti	Oct. 12, 1836
Signora Rossi	May 12, 1837
Mme Caradon-Allen	Mar. 12, 1838
Mrs. Seguin	Dec. 5, 1839
Miss Poole	Feb. 8, 1841
Mme Castellan	Dec. 14, 1843
Signora Euphrasia-Borghese	April 12, 1844
Signora Pico	Jan'y 28, 1845
Mad. Anna Bishop	Jan'y 1, 1848
Mad. Tedesso	Mar. 14, 1848
Signora Truffi	Mar. 25, 1848
Signora Amalia Patti	Mar. 25, 1848
Signora Biscaccianti	Mar. 25, 1848
Signora Lietti-Corsi	Mar. 25, 1848
Mad. Amanda Burton	Oct. 15, 1848
Mme. Laborde	Oct. 17, 1848
Mad. Bertucca	May 30, 1850
Miss Caroline Pintard	May 30, 1850
Mme. Theresa Parodi	Jan'y 1, 1851
Signora Angiolina	April 24, 1851
Miss Catharine Hayes	Dec. 6, 1851
Mad. Amalia Strakosch	June 3, 1852
Signorina Adelina Patti	Sept. 21, 1852
Mme. Marietta Alboni	Sept. 27, 1852
Mme Henrietta Sontag	Oct. 14, 1852
Mdlle. Tourny	Dec 3, 1852
Miss Jenny Lind	Oct 18, 1855
Miss Jenny Lind	Oct. 19, 1855
Miss Jenny Lind	Nov. 27, 1855
Miss Jenny Lind	Nov. 29, 1855
Miss Jenny Lind	Nov. 30, 1855
Miss Jenny Lind	Dec. 16, 1855
Miss Jenny Lind	Dec. 19, 1855
Miss Jenny Lind	Dec. 22, 1855

Mad. Grisi	Jan'y 10, 1855
Mad. Vestvali	Sept. 29, 1855
Miss Louisa Pyne	Sept. 29, 1855
Mad. La Grange	June 6, 1855
Mad. Gazzaniga	April 25, 1857
Mad. Isidora Clark	May 28, 1857
Mad. D'Angri	Sept. 25, 1857
Mad. Frezzolini	Nov. 13, 1857

Signor Fornisari	Mar. 7, 1833
Signor Corsetti	Mar. 7, 1833
Signor Pedrotti	Mar. 7, 1833
Mr. Wood	Feb. 26, 1834
Signor Valletina	May 12, 1837
Signor Natale Felice	May 12, 1837
Signor Brough	Mar. 12, 1838
Mr. Henry Russell	Mar. 12, 1838
Mr. Seguin	Oct. 30, 1839
Signor Grampietro	Dec. 14, 1840
Signor Luigi Perozzi	April 12, 1844
Signor Antognini	Jan'y 28, 1845
Signor Sanquirico	Jan'y 28, 1845
Mr. Templeton	Sept. 28, 1845
Signor Beneventano	Mar. 25, 1848
Signor Rossi	Mar. 25, 1848
Signor Corsi	Mar 25, 1848
Signor Benedetti	Mar. 25, 1848
Signor Avignone	Mar. 25, 1848
Signor Bellini	Mar 25, 1848
Signor Vietti	April 3, 1848
Signor Novello	April 3, 1848
Signor Halma	April 3, 1848
Signor Natale Perelli	May 25, 1848
Signor Debreul	Oct. 7, 1848
Signor Arnoldi	Oct. 7, 1848
Signor Giubelei	Oct. 7, 1848
Signor La Borde	Oct 17, 1848
Signor Lorini	Jan'y 1, 1851
Signor Bettini	April 24, 1851
Signor Badiali	April 24, 1851
Signor Bosio	April 24, 1851
Signor Marini	April 24, 1851
Signor Colletti	April 24, 1851
Signor Baritini	April 24, 1851
Signor Martinelli	April 24, 1851
Signor Strini	April 24, 1851
Signor Condi	April 24, 1851
Signor Pozzolini	Dec. 11, 1853
Signor Rocco	Nov. 26, 1852
Signor Cortesi	Dec. 3, 1852
Signor Mario	Jan'y 10, 1855
Signor Ceresa	Sept. 29, 1855
Signor Brignoli	Dec. 1, 1855
Signor Amodio	April 12, 1856
Mr. Wm. Harrison	Sept 29, 1855

Conductors.

Charles F. Hupfeld	1821	G. Schetky	1821
Benjamin Cross	1821	A. Reinhart	1838
Benjamin Carr	1821	Henri Riha	1838
T. Loud	1821	Carl Lenshow	1848

Carl Bergmann 1848	Michael H. Cross . . . .
Max Maretzek 1849	Carl Sentz . . . .
Josef Gungl 1849	Charles M. Schmitz . . . . .
Natale Perelli 1849	Simon Hassler . . . .
Leopold Meignen 1850	Mark Hassler . . . .
Maurice Strakosch 1851	Wm. Stoll, Jr. . . . .

Solo Violinists.

Signor Rapetti 1837	Paul Julien 1852
Herr H. 1841	Guiseppe Foghel 1852
Herr Nagel 1841	Vieuxtemps . . . .
Mr. Bley 1843	Kopta . . . .
Signor Artot 1843	Carl Gaertner 1846
Ole Bull 1844	Arditi 1847
Camilla Sivori 1846	Louis Gaertner . . . .
Carl Hohnstock 1849	Simon Hassler . . . .
Griebel 1851	Wm. Stoll, Jr. . . . .
Hausser 1852	

Solo Violoncellists.

Mr. Gilles 1821	Signor Casella 1844
Mr. Schindielecker 1829	Mr. Chas. M. Schmitz . . . 1851
Mr. Knoop 1841	Mr. Rudolph Hennig 1869
Walteufel	

Solo Pianists.

Kossowski 1840	Thalberg 1857
Leopold De Meyer 1846	Jarvis 1844
Henri Herz 1846	Carl Wolfsohn . . . .
Maurice Strakosch 1847	Gustave Satter . . . .
Alfred Jaell 1852	Bonnewitz . . . .
L. Moreau Gottschalk 1853	

Rental of Hall—Schedule of Prices.

BALLS, including Banquet-Room and Parlors, ... until 3 o'clock A. M., precisely . . . . $ 85
BALLS, including Banquet-Room and Parlors, ... until 2 o'clock A. M., precisely 75
BALLS, including Banquet-Room only . . . . until 3 o'clock A. M., precisely 75
BALLS, including Banquet-Room only . . . . until 2 o'clock A. M., precisely 65
BALLS, including Banquet-Room (with concert previous) . . . . until 2 o'clock A. M., precisely 70
BALLS, without Banquet-Room or Parlors . . . . until 3 o'clock A. M., precisely 60
BALLS, without Banquet-Room or Parlors . . . . until 2 o'clock A. M., precisely 50
CONCERTS, LECTURES, OR READINGS . . . . until 10 o'clock P. M., precisely 40
CONCERTS, LECTURES, OR READINGS . . . . until 10.30 o'clock P. M., precisely 45
CONCERTS, LECTURES, OR READINGS . . . . until 11 o'clock P. M., precisely 50
DINNERS, OR SUPPERS, in Main Saloon . . . . until 2 o'clock A. M., precisely 100
DINNERS, OR SUPPERS, in Banquet-Room . . . . until 2 o'clock A. M., precisely 50
BUSINESS MEETINGS, in Main Saloon . . . . until 9.45 o'clock P. M., precisely 30
BUSINESS MEETINGS, in Banquet-Room . . . . until 9.45 o'clock P. M., precisely 20
COMMENCEMENTS, OR MEETINGS, Main Saloon (day-time) . . . . until 4 o'clock P. M., precisely 30
COMMENCEMENTS, OR MEETINGS, Banquet Room (day-time), ... until 4 o'clock P. M., precisely 15

NOTE.—Ten Dollars must be paid when contracts are signed, and balance before 4 o'clock, P. M., on day engaged.
Lights will not be turned on unless rental-price is paid in full.
Lights will be turned off precisely at the hour specified in contracts.
All Balls and Parties must end at 3 o'clock, A. M.
The Hall will not be rented for Balls or Parties when admission tickets are less than fifty cents each.

Programme.

PART I

UNDER MR. WILLIAM STOLL, JR., CONDUCTOR.

---

1. March—" The Iron Cross " . . . . *Isemann*
2. Overture—" Raymond " . . . . *Thomas*
3. Grand Selection—" La Giaconda " . . . . . . *Ponchielli*
4. Waltz—" Return of Spring " . . . . *Waldteufel*
5. Intermezzo—" Schelm Amour " . . . . *Eilenberg*
6. Salterella—" Pechenr Napolitau et Napolitaine "
   Rubinstein
7. Gavotte—" Imperial " . . . . *Hanau*
8. Waltz—" Lagunen " . . . . *Strauss*

PART II.

1. March—" Athalia " . . . . *Mendelssohn*
2. Selection—" Mignon " . . . . *Thomas*
3. Waltz—" Poor Jonathan " . . . . *Millocker*
4. Polish National Dance . . . . *Scharwenka*
5. Reve Apres Bal . . . . *Boustet*
6. Selection—" Paul Jones " . . . . *Planquette*
7. Waltz—" O ! Beautiful May " . . . . *Strauss*
8. Galop—" Gladys " . . . . *Geo. P. Kimball*

www.ingramcontent.com/pod-product-compliance
Lightning Source LLC
Chambersburg PA
CBHW030011030726
47499CB00008B/3001